The Poetry of Stephen Vincent Benet
Young Adventure

Stephen Vincent Bene't (22 July 1898 - 13 March 1943) was from a family with roots in Florida, which explains the Spanish name. Although born in Bethlehem, Pennsylvania, his father was a colonel in the U.S. Army, and hence he grew up in California and Georgia. He attended Yale starting in 1915 and that same year published his first book of poems, `Five Men and Pompey'. `Young Adventure' (1918) is considered his first mature book of poetry, and he went on to win two Pulitzer Prizes, in 1929 for `John Brown's Body' and in 1944 for `Western Star'.

It appears that the whole family had great talents, as his grandfather was a Brigadier General, his father a Colonel, and both Stephen and his brother William Rose Benet won Pulitzer Prizes for poetry.

Index Of Contents

To W. R. B.

Dedication

And so, to you, who always were
Perseus, D'Artagnan, Lancelot
To me, I give these weedy rhymes
In memory of earlier times.
Now all those careless days are not.
Of all my heroes, you endure.

Words are such silly things! too rough,
Too smooth, they boil up or congeal,
And neither of us likes emotion
But I can't measure my devotion!
And you know how I really feel
And we're together. There, enough,...!

Foreword by Chauncey Brewster Tinker

In these days when the old civilisation is crumbling beneath our feet, the thought of poetry crosses the mind like the dear memory of things that have long since passed away. In our passionate desire for the new era, it is difficult to refrain oneself from the commonplace practice of speculating on the effects of warfare and of prophesying all manner of novel rebirths. But it may be well for us to remember that the era which has recently closed was itself marked by a mad idealisation of all novelties. In the literary movements of the last decade, when, indeed, any movement at all has been perceptible, we have witnessed a bewildering rise and fall of methods and ideals. We were captivated for a time by the quest of the golden phrase and the accompanying cultivation of exotic emotions; and then, wearying of the pretty and the temperamental, we plunged into the bloodshot brutalities of naturalism.

From the smooth-flowing imitations of Tennyson and Swinburne, we passed into a false freedom that had at its heart a repudiation of all law and standards, for a parallel to which one turns instinctively to certain recent developments in the political world. We may hope that the eager search for novelty of form and subject may have its influence in releasing us from our old bondage to the commonplace and in broadening the scope of poetry; but we cannot blind ourselves to the fact that it has at the same time completed that estrangement between the poet and the general public which has been developing for half a century. The great mass of the reading world, to whom the arts should minister, have now forgotten that poetry is a consolation in times of doubt and peril, a beacon, and "an ever-fixed mark" in a crazed and shifting world. Our poetry, and I am speaking in particular of American poetry, has been centrifugal; our poets have broken up into smaller and ever smaller groups. Individualism has triumphed.

To the general confusion, critics, if they may be said to have existed at all, have added by their paltry conception of the art. They have deemed it a sufficient denunciation of a poet to accuse him of imitating his masters; as though the history of an art were rather a series of violent rebellions than a growth and a progressive illumination. Not all generations are privileged to see the working of a great creative impulse, but the want, keen though it be, furnishes no reason for the utter rejection of

A tremulous murmur from great days long dead.

But this fear of echoing the past may work us a yet greater misfortune. In the rejection of the manner of an earlier epoch may be implicit also the rejection of the very sources from which springs the life of the fair art. Melody, and a love of the green earth, and a yearning for God are of the very fabric of poetry, deny it who will. The Muses still reign on Parnassus, wax the heathen never so furious. Poets who love poetry better than their own fame in Grub Street will do well to remember

The flame, the noble pageant of our life;
The burning seal that stamps man's high indenture
To vain attempt and most forlorn adventure;
Romance and purple seas, and toppling towns,
And the wind's valiance crying o'er the downs.

It is a poor business to find in such words only the illusions of youth and a new enthusiasm. The desire for novelty, the passion for force and dirt, and the hankering after freakishness of mood, which many have attempted to substitute for the older and simpler things, are themselves the best evidence of disillusion and jaded nerves. There is a weariness and a disgust in our recent impatience with beauty which indicate too clearly the exhaustion of our spiritual resources. It may well be that the rebirth of poetry is to be manifest in a reappearance of the obvious, in a love of the sea and of the beauty of clouds, in the adventure of death and the yet more amazing adventure of living, in a vital love of colour, whether of the Orient or the drug-shop, in childlike love of melody, and the cool cleansing of rain, in strange faces and old memories. This, in the past, has been poetry, and this will be poetry again. The singer who, out of a full heart, can offer to the world his vision of its beauty, and out of a noble mind, his conception of its destiny, will bestow upon his time the most precious gift which we can now receive, the gift of his healing power.

C. B. T.

I. The Drug-Shop, or, Endymion in Edmonstoun

Prefatory Note.

This poem received the nineteenth award of the prize offered by Professor Albert Stanburrough Cook to Yale University for the best unpublished verse, the Committee of Award consisting of Professors C. F. Tucker Brooke, of Yale University, Robert Frost, of Amherst College, and Charles M. Gayley, of the University of California.

"Oh yes, I went over to Edmonstoun the other day and saw
Johnny, mooning around as usual! He will never make his way."
Letter of George Keats, 18--

Night falls; the great jars glow against the dark,
Dark green, dusk red, and, like a coiling snake,
Writhing eternally in smoky gyres,
Great ropes of gorgeous vapor twist and turn
Within them. So the Eastern fisherman
Saw the swart genie rise when the lead seal,
Scribbled with charms, was lifted from the jar;
And - well, how went the tale? Like this, like this?...

No herbage broke the barren flats of land,
No winds dared loiter within smiling trees,
Nor were there any brooks on either hand,
Only the dry, bright sand,
Naked and golden, lay before the seas.

One boat toiled noiselessly along the deep,
The thirsty ripples dying silently
Upon its track. Far out the brown nets sweep,
And night begins to creep
Across the intolerable mirror of the sea.

Twice the nets rise, a-trail with sea-plants brown,
Distorted shells, and rocks green-mossed with slime,
Nought else. The fisher, sick at heart, kneels down;
"Prayer may appease God's frown,"
He thinks, then, kneeling, casts for the third time.

And lo! an earthen jar, bound round with brass,
Lies tangled in the cordage of his net.
About the bright waves gleam like shattered glass,
And where the sea's rim was
The sun dips, flat and red, about to set.

The prow grates on the beach. The fisherman
Stoops, tearing at the cords that bind the seal.
Shall pearls roll out, lustrous and white and wan?
Lapis? carnelian?
Unheard-of stones that make the sick mind reel

With wonder of their beauty? Rubies, then?
Green emeralds, glittering like the eyes of beasts?
Poisonous opals, good to madden men?
Gold bezants, ten and ten?
Hard, regal diamonds, like kingly feasts?

He tugged; the seal gave way. A little smoke

Curled like a feather in the darkening sky.
A blinding gush of fire burst, flamed, and broke.
A voice like a wind spoke.
Armored with light, and turbaned terribly,

A genie tramped the round earth underfoot;
His head sought out the stars, his cupped right hand
Made half the sky one darkness. He was mute.
The sun, a ripened fruit,
Drooped lower. Scarlet eddied o'er the sand.

The genie spoke: "O miserable one!
Thy prize awaits thee; come, and hug it close!
A noble crown thy draggled nets have won
For this that thou hast done.
Blessed are fools! A gift remains for those!"

His hand sought out his sword, and lightnings flared
Across the sky in one great bloom of fire.
Poised like a toppling mountain, it hung bared;
Suns that were jewels glared
Along its hilt. The air burnt like a pyre.

Once more the genie spoke: "Something I owe
To thee, thou fool, thou fool. Come, canst thou sing?
Yea? Sing then; if thy song be brave, then go
Free and released - or no!
Find first some task, some overmastering thing
I cannot do, and find it speedily,
For if thou dost not thou shalt surely die!"

The sword whirled back. The fisherman uprose,
And if at first his voice was weak with fear
And his limbs trembled, it was but a doze,
And at the high song's close
He stood up straight. His voice rang loud and clear.

The Song

Last night the quays were lighted;
Cressets of smoking pine
Glared o'er the roaring mariners
That drink the yellow wine.

Their song rolled to the rafters,
It struck the high stars pale,
Such worth was in their discourse,
Such wonder in their tale.

Blue borage filled the clinking cups,
The murky night grew wan,
Till one rose, crowned with laurel-leaves,
That was an outland man.

"Come, let us drink to war!" said he,
"The torch of the sacked town!
The swan's-bath and the wolf-ships,
And Harald of renown!

"Yea, while the milk was on his lips,
Before the day was born,
He took the Almayne Kaiser's head
To be his drinking-horn!

"Yea, while the down was on his chin,
Or yet his beard was grown,
He broke the gates of Micklegarth,
And stole the lion-throne!

"Drink to Harald, king of the world,
Lord of the tongue and the troth!
To the bellowing horns of Ostfriesland,
And the trumpets of the Goth!"

Their shouts rolled to the rafters,
The drink-horns crashed and rang,
And all their talk was a clangor of war,
As swords together sang!

But dimly, through the deep night,
Where stars like flowers shone,
A passionate shape came gliding
I saw one thing alone.

I only saw my young love
Shining against the dark,
The whiteness of her raiment,
The head that bent to hark.

I only saw my young love,
Like flowers in the sun
Her hands like waxen petals,
Where yawning poppies run.

I only felt there, chrysmal,
Against my cheek her breath,
Though all the winds were baying,
And the sky bright with Death.

Red sparks whirled up the chimney,

A hungry flaught of flame,
And a lean man from Greece arose;
Thrasyllos was his name.

"I praise all noble wines!" he cried,
"Green robes of tissue fine,
Peacocks and apes and ivory,
And Homer's sea-loud line,

"Statues and rings and carven gems,
And the wise crawling sea;
But most of all the crowns of kings,
The rule they wield thereby!

"Power, fired power, blank and bright!
A fit hilt for the hand!
The one good sword for a freeman,
While yet the cold stars stand!"

Their shouts rolled to the rafters,
The air was thick with wine.
I only knew her deep eyes,
And felt her hand in mine.

Softly as quiet water,
One finger touched my cheek;
Her face like gracious moonlight
I might not move nor speak.

I only saw that beauty,
I only felt that form
There, in the silken darkness
God wot my heart was warm!

Their shouts rolled to the rafters,
Another chief began;
His slit lips showed him for a Hun;
He was an evil man.

"Sing to the joys of women!" he yelled,
"The hot delicious tents,
The soft couch, and the white limbs;
The air a steam of scents!"

His eyes gleamed, and he wet his lips,
The rafters shook with cheers,
As he sang of woman, who is man's slave
For all unhonored years.

"Whether the wanton laughs amain,
With one white shoulder bare,

Or in a sacked room you unbind
Some crouching maiden's hair;

"This is the only good for man,
Like spices of the South
To see the glimmering body laid
As pasture to his mouth!

"To leave no lees within the cup,
To see and take and rend;
To lap a girl's limbs up like wine,
And laugh, knowing the end!"

Only, like low, still breathing,
I heard one voice, one word;
And hot speech poured upon my lips,
As my hands held a sword.

"Fools, thrice fools of lust!" I cried,
"Your eyes are blind to see
Eternal beauty, moving far,
More glorious than horns of war!
But though my eyes were one blind scar,
That sight is shown to me!

"You nuzzle at the ivory side,
You clasp the golden head;
Fools, fools, who chatter and sing,
You have taken the sign of a terrible thing,
You have drunk down God with your beeswing,
And broken the saints for bread!

"For God moves darkly,
In silence and in storm;
But in the body of woman
He shows one burning form.

"For God moves blindly,
In darkness and in dread;
But in the body of woman
He raises up the dead.

"Gracile and straight as birches,
Swift as the questing birds,
They fill true-lovers' drink-horns up,
Who speak not, having no words.

"Love is not delicate toying,
A slim and shimmering mesh;
It is two souls wrenched into one,
Two bodies made one flesh.

"Lust is a sprightly servant,
Gallant where wines are poured;
Love is a bitter master,
Love is an iron lord.

"Satin ease of the body,
Fattened sloth of the hands,
These and their like he will not send,
Only immortal fires to rend
And the world's end is your journey's end,
And your stream chokes in the sands.

"Pleached calms shall not await you,
Peace you shall never find;
Nought but the living moorland
Scourged naked by the wind.

"Nought but the living moorland,
And your love's hand in yours;
The strength more sure than surety,
The mercy that endures.

"Then, though they give you to be burned,
And slay you like a stoat,
You have found the world's heart in the turn of a cheek,
Heaven in the lift of a throat.

"Although they break you on the wheel,
That stood so straight in the sun,
Behind you the trumpets split the sky,
Where the lost and furious fight goes by
And God, our God, will have victory
When the red day is done!"

Their mirth rolled to the rafters,
They bellowed lechery;
Light as a drifting feather
My love slipped from my knee.

Within, the lights were yellow
In drowsy rooms and warm;
Without, the stabbing lightning
Shattered across the storm.

Within, the great logs crackled,
The drink-horns emptied soon;
Without, the black cloaks of the clouds
Strangled the waning moon.

My love crossed o'er the threshold

God! but the night was murk!
I set myself against the cold,
And left them to their work.

Their shouts rolled to the rafters;
A bitterer way was mine,
And I left them in the tavern,
Drinking the yellow wine!

The last faint echoes rang along the plains,
Died, and were gone. The genie spoke: "Thy song
Serves well enough - but yet thy task remains;
Many and rending pains
Shall torture him who dares delay too long!"

His brown face hardened to a leaden mask.
A bitter brine crusted the fisher's cheek
"Almighty God, one thing alone I ask,
Show me a task, a task!"
The hard cup of the sky shone, gemmed and bleak.

"O love, whom I have sought by devious ways;
O hidden beauty, naked as a star;
You whose bright hair has burned across my days,
Making them lamps of praise;
O dawn-wind, breathing of Arabia!

"You have I served. Now fire has parched the vine,
And Death is on the singers and the song.
No longer are there lips to cling to mine,
And the heart wearies of wine,
And I am sick, for my desire is long.

"O love, soft-moving, delicate and tender!
In her gold house the pipe calls querulously,
They cloud with thin green silks her body slender,
They talk to her and tend her;
Come, piteous, gentle love, and set me free!"

He ceased - and, slowly rising o'er the deep,
A faint song chimed, grew clearer, till at last
A golden horn of light began to creep
Where the dumb ripples sweep,
Making the sea one splendor where it passed.

A golden boat! The bright oars rested soon,
And the prow met the sand. The purple veils
Misting the cabin fell. Fair as the moon
When the morning comes too soon,
And all the air is silver in the dales,

A gold-robed princess stepped upon the beach.
The fisher knelt and kissed her garment's hem,
And then her lips, and strove at last for speech.
The waters lapped the reach.
"Here thy strength breaks, thy might is nought to stem!"

He cried at last. Speech shook him like a flame:
"Yea, though thou plucked the stars from out the sky,
Each lovely one would be a withered shame
Each thou couldst find or name
To this fire-hearted beauty!" Wearily

The genie heard. A slow smile came like dawn
Over his face. "Thy task is done!" he said.
A whirlwind roared, smoke shattered, he was gone;
And, like a sudden horn,
The moon shone clear, no longer smoked and red.

They passed into the boat. The gold oars beat
Loudly, then fainter, fainter, till at last
Only the quiet waters barely moved
Along the whispering sand - till all the vast
Expanse of sea began to shake with heat,
And morning brought soft airs, by sailors loved.

And after?... Well...
The shop-bell clangs! Who comes?
Quinine - I pour the little bitter grains
Out upon blue, glazed squares of paper. So.
And all the dusk I shall sit here alone,
With many powers in my hands - ah, see
How the blurred labels run on the old jars!
Opium - and a cruel and sleepy scent,
The harsh taste of white poppies; India
The writhing woods a-crawl with monstrous life,
Save where the deodars are set like spears,
And a calm pool is mirrored ebony;
Opium - brown and warm and slender-breasted
She rises, shaking off the cool black water,
And twisting up her hair, that ripples down,
A torrent of black water, to her feet;
How the drops sparkle in the moonlight! Once
I made a rhyme about it, singing softly:

Over Damascus every star
Keeps his unchanging course and cold,
The dark weighs like an iron bar,
The intense and pallid night is old,
Dim the moon's scimitar.

Still the lamps blaze within those halls,

Where poppies heap the marble vats
For girls to tread; the thick air palls;
And shadows hang like evil bats
About the scented walls.

The girls are many, and they sing;
Their white feet fall like flakes of snow,
Making a ceaseless murmuring
Whispers of love, dead long ago,
And dear, forgotten Spring.

One alone sings not. Tiredly
She sees the white blooms crushed, and smells
The heavy scent. They chatter: "See!
White Zira thinks of nothing else
But the morn's jollity

"Then Haroun takes her!" But she dreams,
Unhearing, of a certain field
Of poppies, cut by many streams,
Like lines across a round Turk shield,
Where now the hot sun gleams.

The field whereon they walked that day,
And splendor filled her body up,
And his; and then the trampled clay,
And slow smoke climbing the sky's cup
From where the village lay.

And after - much ache of the wrists,
Where the cords irked her - till she came,
The price of many amethysts,
Hither. And now the ultimate shame
Blew trumpet in the lists.

And so she trod the poppies there,
Remembering other poppies, too,
And did not seem to see or care.
Without, the first gray drops of dew
Sweetened the trembling air.

She trod the poppies. Hours passed
Until she slept at length - and Time
Dragged his slow sickle. When at last
She woke, the moon shone, bright as rime,
And night's tide rolled on fast.

She moaned once, knowing everything;
Then, bitterer than death, she found
The soft handmaidens, in a ring,
Come to anoint her, all around,

That she might please the king.

Opium - and the odor dies away,
Leaving the air yet heavy - cassia - myrrh
Bitter and splendid. See, the poisons come,
Trooping in squat green vials, blazoned red
With grinning skulls: strychnine, a pallid dust
Of tiny grains, like bones ground fine; and next
The muddy green of arsenic, all livid,
Likest the face of one long dead - they creep
Along the dusty shelf like deadly beetles,
Whose fangs are carved with runnels, that the blood
May run down easily to the blind mouth
That snaps and gapes; and high above them there,
My master's pride, a cobwebbed, yellow pot
Of honey from Mount Hybla. Do the bees
Still moan among the low sweet purple clover,
Endlessly many? Still in deep-hushed woods,
When the incredible silver of the moon
Comes like a living wind through sleep-bowed branches,
Still steal dark shapes from the enchanted glens,
Which yet are purple with high dreams, and still
Fronting that quiet and eternal shield
Which is much more than Peace, does there still stand
One sharp black shadow - and the short, smooth horns
Are clear against that disk?
O great Diana!
I, I have praised thee, yet I do not know
What moves my mind so strangely, save that once
I lay all night upon a thymy hill,
And watched the slow clouds pass like heaped-up foam
Across blue marble, till at last no speck
Blotted the clear expanse, and the full moon
Rose in much light, and all night long I saw
Her ordered progress, till, in midmost heaven,
There came a terrible silence, and the mice
Crept to their holes, the crickets did not chirp,
All the small night-sounds stopped - and clear pure light
Rippled like silk over the universe,
Most cold and bleak; and yet my heart beat fast,
Waiting until the stillness broke. I know not
For what I waited - something very great
I dared not look up to the sky for fear
A brittle crackling should clash suddenly
Against the quiet, and a black line creep
Across the sky, and widen like a mouth,
Until the broken heavens streamed apart,
Like torn lost banners, and the immortal fires,
Roaring like lions, asked their meat from God.
I lay there, a black blot upon a shield
Of quivering, watery whiteness. The hush held

Until I staggered up and cried aloud,
And then it seemed that something far too great
For knowledge, and illimitable as God,
Rent the dark sky like lightning, and I fell,
And, falling, heard a wild and rushing wind
Of music, and saw lights that blinded me
With white, impenetrable swords, and felt
A pressure of soft hands upon my lips,
Upon my eyelids - and since then I cough
At times, and have strange thoughts about the stars,
That some day - some day
Come, I must be quick!
My master will be back soon. Let me light
Thin blue Arabian pastilles, and sit
Like a dead god incensed by chanting priests,
And watch the pungent smoke wreathe up and up,
Until he comes - though he may rage because
They cost good money. Then I shall walk home
Over the moor. Already the moon climbs
Above the world's edge. By the time he comes
She will be fully risen. There's his step!

II. Miscellaneous.

Rain After a Vaudeville Show

The last pose flickered, failed. The screen's dead white
Glared in a sudden flooding of harsh light
Stabbing the eyes; and as I stumbled out
The curtain rose. A fat girl with a pout
And legs like hams, began to sing "His Mother".
Gusts of bad air rose in a choking smother;
Smoke, the wet steam of clothes, the stench of plush,
Powder, cheap perfume, mingled in a rush.
I stepped into the lobby and stood still
Struck dumb by sudden beauty, body and will.
Cleanness and rapture - excellence made plain
The storming, thrashing arrows of the rain!
Pouring and dripping on the roofs and rods,
Smelling of woods and hills and fresh-turned sods,
Black on the sidewalks, gray in the far sky,
Crashing on thirsty panes, on gutters dry,
Hurrying the crowd to shelter, making fair
The streets, the houses, and the heat-soaked air,
Merciful, holy, charging, sweeping, flashing,
It smote the soul with a most iron clashing!...
Like dragons' eyes the street-lamps suddenly gleamed,
Yellow and round and dim-low globes of flame.
And, scarce-perceived, the clouds' tall banners streamed.

Out of the petty wars, the daily shame,
Beauty strove suddenly, and rose, and flowered....
I gripped my coat and plunged where awnings lowered.
Made one with hissing blackness, caught, embraced,
By splendor and by striving and swift haste
Spring coming in with thunderings and strife
I stamped the ground in the strong joy of life!

The City Revisited

The grey gulls drift across the bay
Softly and still as flakes of snow
Against the thinning fog. All day
I sat and watched them come and go;
And now at last the sun was set,
Filling the waves with colored fire
Till each seemed like a jewelled spire
Thrust up from some drowned city. Soon
From peak and cliff and minaret
The city's lights began to wink,
Each like a friendly word. The moon
Began to broaden out her shield,
Spurting with silver. Straight before
The brown hills lay like quiet beasts
Stretched out beside a well-loved door,
And filling earth and sky and field
With the calm heaving of their breasts.

Nothing was gone, nothing was changed,
The smallest wave was unestranged
By all the long ache of the years
Since last I saw them, blind with tears.
Their welcome like the hills stood fast:
And I, I had come home at last.

So I laughed out with them aloud
To think that now the sun was broad,
And climbing up the iron sky,
Where the raw streets stretched sullenly
About another room I knew,
In a mean house - and soon there, too,
The smith would burst the flimsy door
And find me lying on the floor.
Just where I fell the other night,
After that breaking wave of pain.
How they will storm and rage and fight,
Servants and mistress, one and all,
"No money for the funeral!"

I broke my life there. Let it stand
At that.
The waters are a plain,
Heaving and bright on either hand,
A tremulous and lustral peace
Which shall endure though all things cease,
Filling my heart as water fills
A cup. There stand the quiet hills.
So, waiting for my wings to grow,
I watch the gulls sail to and fro,
Rising and falling, soft and swift,
Drifting along as bubbles drift.
And, though I see the face of God
Hereafter - this day have I trod
Nearer to Him than I shall tread
Ever again. The night is dead.
And there's the dawn, poured out like wine
Along the dim horizon-line.
And from the city comes the chimes

We have our heaven on earth - sometimes!

Going Back to School

The boat ploughed on. Now Alcatraz was past
And all the grey waves flamed to red again
At the dead sun's last glimmer. Far and vast
The Sausalito lights burned suddenly
In little dots and clumps, as if a pen
Had scrawled vague lines of gold across the hills;
The sky was like a cup some rare wine fills,
And stars came as he watched
- and he was free
One splendid instant - back in the great room,
Curled in a chair with all of them beside
And the whole world a rush of happy voices,
With laughter beating in a clamorous tide....
Saw once again the heat of harvest fume
Up to the empty sky in threads like glass,
And ran, and was a part of what rejoices
In thunderous nights of rain; lay in the grass
Sun-baked and tired, looking through a maze
Of tiny stems into a new green world;
Once more knew eves of perfume, days ablaze
With clear, dry heat on the brown, rolling fields;
Shuddered with fearful ecstasy in bed
Over a book of knights and bloody shields...
The ship slowed, jarred and stopped. There, straight ahead,
Were dock and fellows. Stumbling, he was whirled

Out and away to meet them - and his back
Slumped to the old half-cringe, his hands fell slack;
A big boy's arm went round him - and a twist
Sent shattering pain along his tortured wrist,
As a voice cried, a bloated voice and fat,
"Why it's Miss Nancy! Come along, you rat!"

Nos Immortales

Perhaps we go with wind and cloud and sun,
Into the free companionship of air;
Perhaps with sunsets when the day is done,
All's one to me - I do not greatly care;
So long as there are brown hills - and a tree
Like a mad prophet in a land of dearth
And I can lie and hear eternally
The vast monotonous breathing of the earth.

I have known hours, slow and golden-glowing,
Lovely with laughter and suffused with light,
O Lord, in such a time appoint my going,
When the hands clench, and the cold face grows white,
And the spark dies within the feeble brain,
Spilling its star-dust back to dust again.

Young Blood

"But, sir," I said, "they tell me the man is like to die!"
The Canon shook his head indulgently.
"Young blood, Cousin," he boomed.
"Young blood! Youth will be served!"
D'Hermonville's Fabliaux.

He woke up with a sick taste in his mouth
And lay there heavily, while dancing motes
Whirled through his brain in endless, rippling streams,
And a grey mist weighed down upon his eyes
So that they could not open fully. Yet
After some time his blurred mind stumbled back
To its last ragged memory - a room;
Air foul with wine; a shouting, reeling crowd
Of friends who dragged him, dazed and blind with drink
Out to the street; a crazy rout of cabs;
The steady mutter of his neighbor's voice,
Mumbling out dull obscenity by rote;
And then... well, they had brought him home it seemed,
Since he awoke in bed - oh, damn the business!

He had not wanted it - the silly jokes,
"One last, great night of freedom ere you're married!"
"You'll get no fun then!" "H-ssh, don't tell that story!
He'll have a wife soon!" - God! the sitting down
To drink till you were sodden!...
Like great light
She came into his thoughts. That was the worst.
To wallow in the mud like this because
His friends were fools.... He was not fit to touch,
To see, oh far, far off, that silver place
Where God stood manifest to man in her....
Fouling himself.... One thing he brought to her,
At least. He had been clean; had taken it
A kind of point of honor from the first...
Others might do it... but he didn't care
For those things....
Suddenly his vision cleared.
And something seemed to grow within his mind....
Something was wrong - the color of the wall
The queer shape of the bedposts - everything
Was changed, somehow... his room. Was this his room?

... He turned his head and saw beside him there
The sagging body's slope, the paint-smeared face,
And the loose, open mouth, lax and awry,
The breasts, the bleached and brittle hair... these things.
... As if all Hell were crushed to one bright line
Of lightning for a moment. Then he sank,
Prone beneath an intolerable weight.
And bitter loathing crept up all his limbs.

The Quality of Courage

Black trees against an orange sky,
Trees that the wind shook terribly,
Like a harsh spume along the road,
Quavering up like withered arms,
Writhing like streams, like twisted charms
Of hot lead flung in snow. Below
The iron ice stung like a goad,
Slashing the torn shoes from my feet,
And all the air was bitter sleet.

And all the land was cramped with snow,
Steel-strong and fierce and glimmering wan,
Like pale plains of obsidian.
And yet I strove - and I was fire
And ice - and fire and ice were one
In one vast hunger of desire.

A dim desire, of pleasant places,
And lush fields in the summer sun,
And logs aflame, and walls, and faces,
And wine, and old ambrosial talk,
A golden ball in fountains dancing,
And unforgotten hands. (Ah, God,
I trod them down where I have trod,
And they remain, and they remain,
Etched in unutterable pain,
Loved lips and faces now apart,
That once were closer than my heart
In agony, in agony,
And horribly a part of me....
For Lethe is for no man set,
And in Hell may no man forget.)

And there were flowers, and jugs, bright-glancing,
And old Italian swords - and looks,
A moment's glance of fire, of fire,
Spiring, leaping, flaming higher,
Into the intense, the cloudless blue,
Until two souls were one, and flame,
And very flesh, and yet the same!
As if all springs were crushed anew
Into one globed drop of dew!
But for the most I thought of heat,
Desiring greatly.... Hot white sand
The lazy body lies at rest in,
Or sun-dried, scented grass to nest in,
And fires, innumerable fires,
Great fagots hurling golden gyres
Of sparks far up, and the red heart
In sea-coals, crashing as they part
To tiny flares, and kindling snapping,
Bunched sticks that burst their string and wrapping
And fall like jackstraws; green and blue
The evil flames of driftwood too,
And heavy, sullen lumps of coke
With still, fierce heat and ugly smoke....
And then the vision of his face,
And theirs, all theirs, came like a sword,
Thrice, to the heart - and as I fell
I thought I saw a light before.

I woke. My hands were blue and sore,
Torn on the ice. I scarcely felt
The frozen sleet begin to melt
Upon my face as I breathed deeper,
But lay there warmly, like a sleeper
Who shifts his arm once, and moans low,
And then sinks back to night. Slow, slow,

And still as Death, came Sleep and Death
And looked at me with quiet breath.
Unbending figures, black and stark
Against the intense deeps of the dark.
Tall and like trees. Like sweet and fire
Rest crept and crept along my veins,
Gently. And there were no more pains....

Was it not better so to lie?
The fight was done. Even gods tire
Of fighting.... My way was the wrong.
Now I should drift and drift along
To endless quiet, golden peace...
And let the tortured body cease.

And then a light winked like an eye.
And very many miles away
A girl stood at a warm, lit door,
Holding a lamp. Ray upon ray
It cloaked the snow with perfect light.
And where she was there was no night
Nor could be, ever. God is sure,
And in his hands are things secure.
It is not given me to trace
The lovely laughter of that face,
Like a clear brook most full of light,
Or olives swaying on a height,
So silver they have wings, almost;
Like a great word once known and lost
And meaning all things. Nor her voice
A happy sound where larks rejoice,
Her body, that great loveliness,
The tender fashion of her dress,
I may not paint them.
These I see,
Blazing through all eternity,
A fire-winged sign, a glorious tree!

She stood there, and at once I knew
The bitter thing that I must do.
There could be no surrender now;
Though Sleep and Death were whispering low.
My way was wrong. So. Would it mend
If I shrank back before the end?
And sank to death and cowardice?
No, the last lees must be drained up,
Base wine from an ignoble cup;
(Yet not so base as sleek content
When I had shrunk from punishment)
The wretched body strain anew!
Life was a storm to wander through.

I took the wrong way. Good and well,
At least my feet sought out not Hell!
Though night were one consuming flame
I must go on for my base aim,
And so, perhaps, make evil grow
To something clean by agony...
And reach that light upon the snow...
And touch her dress at last...
So, so,
I crawled. I could not speak or see
Save dimly. The ice glared like fire,
A long bright Hell of choking cold,
And each vein was a tautened wire,
Throbbing with torture - and I crawled.
My hands were wounds.
So I attained
The second Hell. The snow was stained
I thought, and shook my head at it
How red it was! Black tree-roots clutched
And tore - and soon the snow was smutched
Anew; and I lurched babbling on,
And then fell down to rest a bit,
And came upon another Hell...
Loose stones that ice made terrible,
That rolled and gashed men as they fell.
I stumbled, slipped... and all was gone
That I had gained. Once more I lay
Before the long bright Hell of ice.
And still the light was far away.
There was red mist before my eyes
Or I could tell you how I went
Across the swaying firmament,
A glittering torture of cold stars,
And how I fought in Titan wars...
And died... and lived again upon
The rack... and how the horses strain
When their red task is nearly done....

I only know that there was Pain,
Infinite and eternal Pain.
And that I fell - and rose again.

So she was walking in the road.
And I stood upright like a man,
Once, and fell blind, and heard her cry...
And then there came long agony.
There was no pain when I awoke,
No pain at all. Rest, like a goad,
Spurred my eyes open - and light broke
Upon them like a million swords:
And she was there. There are no words.

Heaven is for a moment's span.
And ever.
So I spoke and said,
"My honor stands up unbetrayed,
And I have seen you. Dear..."
Sharp pain
Closed like a cloak....
I moaned and died.

Here, even here, these things remain.
I shall draw nearer to her side.

Oh dear and laughing, lost to me,
Hidden in grey Eternity,
I shall attain, with burning feet,
To you and to the mercy-seat!
The ages crumble down like dust,
Dark roses, deviously thrust
And scattered in sweet wine - but I,
I shall lift up to you my cry,
And kiss your wet lips presently
Beneath the ever-living Tree.

This in my heart I keep for goad!
Somewhere, in Heaven she walks that road.
Somewhere... in Heaven... she walks... that... road....

Campus Sonnets:

1. Before an Examination

The little letters dance across the page,
Flaunt and retire, and trick the tired eyes;
Sick of the strain, the glaring light, I rise
Yawning and stretching, full of empty rage
At the dull maunderings of a long dead sage,
Fling up the windows, fling aside his lies;
Choosing to breathe, not stifle and be wise,
And let the air pour in upon my cage.

The breeze blows cool and there are stars and stars
Beyond the dark, soft masses of the elms
That whisper things in windy tones and light.
They seem to wheel for dim, celestial wars;
And I - I hear the clash of silver helms
Ring icy-clear from the far deeps of night.

2. Talk

Tobacco smoke drifts up to the dim ceiling
From half a dozen pipes and cigarettes,
Curling in endless shapes, in blue rings wheeling,
As formless as our talk. Phil, drawling, bets
Cornell will win the relay in a walk,
While Bob and Mac discuss the Giants' chances;
Deep in a morris-chair, Bill scowls at "Falk",
John gives large views about the last few dances.

And so it goes - an idle speech and aimless,
A few chance phrases; yet I see behind
The empty words the gleam of a beauty tameless,
Friendship and peace and fire to strike men blind,
Till the whole world seems small and bright to hold
Of all our youth this hour is pure gold.

3. May Morning

I lie stretched out upon the window-seat
And doze, and read a page or two, and doze,
And feel the air like water on me close,
Great waves of sunny air that lip and beat
With a small noise, monotonous and sweet,
Against the window - and the scent of cool,
Frail flowers by some brown and dew-drenched pool
Possesses me from drowsy head to feet.

This is the time of all-sufficing laughter
At idiotic things some one has done,
And there is neither past nor vague hereafter.
And all your body stretches in the sun
And drinks the light in like a liquid thing;
Filled with the divine languor of late spring.

4. Return - 1917

"The College will reopen Sept. -." `Catalogue'.

I was just aiming at the jagged hole
Torn in the yellow sandbags of their trench,
When something threw me sideways with a wrench,
And the skies seemed to shrivel like a scroll
And disappear... and propped against the bole
Of a big elm I lay, and watched the clouds

Float through the blue, deep sky in speckless crowds,
And I was clean again, and young, and whole.

Lord, what a dream that was! And what a doze
Waiting for Bill to come along to class!
I've cut it now - and he - Oh, hello, Fred!
Why, what's the matter? - here - don't be an ass,
Sit down and tell me! - What do you suppose?
I dreamed I... AM I... wounded? "YOU ARE DEAD."

Alexander VI Dines with the Cardinal of Capua

Next, then, the peacock, gilt
With all its feathers. Look, what gorgeous dyes
Flow in the eyes!
And how deep, lustrous greens are splashed and spilt
Along the back, that like a sea-wave's crest
Scatters soft beauty o'er th' emblazoned breast!

A strange fowl! But most fit
For feasts like this, whereby I honor one
Pure as the sun!
Yet glowing with the fiery zeal of it!
Some wine? Your goblet's empty? Let it foam!
It is not often that you come to Rome!

You like the Venice glass?
Rippled with lines that float like women's curls,
Neck like a girl's,
Fierce-glowing as a chalice in the Mass?
You start - 'twas artist then, not Pope who spoke!
Ave Maria stella! Ah, it broke!

'Tis said they break alone
When poison writhes within. A foolish tale!
What, you look pale?
Caraffa, fetch a silver cup!... You own
A Birth of Venus, now - or so I've heard,
Lovely as the breast-plumage of a bird.

Also a Dancing Faun,
Hewn with the lithe grace of Praxiteles;
Globed pearls to please
A sultan; golden veils that drop like lawn
How happy I could be with but a tithe
Of your possessions, fortunate one! Don't writhe

But take these cushions here!
Now for the fruit! Great peaches, satin-skinned,

Rough tamarind,
Pomegranates red as lips - oh they come dear!
But men like you we feast at any price
A plum perhaps? They're looking rather nice!

I'll cut the thing in half.
There's yours! Now, with a one-side-poisoned knife
One might snuff life
And leave one's friend with - "fool" for epitaph!
An old trick? Truth! But when one has the itch
For pretty things and isn't very rich....

There, eat it all or I'll
Be angry! You feel giddy? Well, it's hot!
This bergamot
Take home and smell - it purges blood of bile!
And when you kiss Bianca's dimpled knee,
Think of the poor Pope in his misery!

Now you may kiss my ring!
Ho there, the Cardinal's litter! - You must dine
When the new wine
Is in, again with me - hear Bice sing,
Even admire my frescoes - though they're nought
Beside the calm Greek glories you have bought!

Godspeed, Sir Cardinal!
And take a weak man's blessing! Help him there
To the cool air!...
Lucrezia here? You're ready for the ball?
He'll die within ten hours, I suppose
MhM! Kiss your poor old father, little rose!

The Breaking Point

It was not when temptation came,
Swiftly and blastingly as flame,
And seared me white with burning scars;
When I stood up for age-long wars
And held the very Fiend at grips;
When all my mutinous body rose
To range itself beside my foes,
And, like a greyhound in the slips,
The Beast that dwells within me roared,
Lunging and straining at his cord....
For all the blusterings of Hell,
It was not then I slipped and fell;
For all the storm, for all the hate,
I kept my soul inviolate!

But when the fight was fought and won,
And there was Peace as still as Death
On everything beneath the sun.
Just as I started to draw breath,
And yawn, and stretch, and pat myself,
The grass began to whisper things
And every tree became an elf,
That grinned and chuckled counsellings:
Birds, beasts, one thing alone they said,
Beating and dinning at my head.
I could not fly. I could not shun it.
Slimily twisting, slow and blind,
It crept and crept into my mind.
Whispered and shouted, sneered and laughed,
Screamed out until my brain was daft....
One snaky word, "WHAT IF YOU'D DONE IT?"

And I began to think...
Ah, well,
What matter how I slipped and fell?
Or you, you gutter-searcher say!
Tell where you found me yesterday!

Lonely Burial

There were not many at that lonely place,
Where two scourged hills met in a little plain.
The wind cried loud in gusts, then low again.
Three pines strained darkly, runners in a race
Unseen by any. Toward the further woods
A dim harsh noise of voices rose and ceased.
We were most silent in those solitudes
Then, sudden as a flame, the black-robed priest,

The clotted earth piled roughly up about
The hacked red oblong of the new-made thing,
Short words in swordlike Latin - and a rout
Of dreams most impotent, unwearying.
Then, like a blind door shut on a carouse,
The terrible bareness of the soul's last house.

Dinner in a Quick Lunch Room

Soup should be heralded with a mellow horn,
Blowing clear notes of gold against the stars;
Strange entrees with a jangle of glass bars

Fantastically alive with subtle scorn;
Fish, by a plopping, gurgling rush of waters,
Clear, vibrant waters, beautifully austere;
Roast, with a thunder of drums to stun the ear,
A screaming fife, a voice from ancient slaughters!

Over the salad let the woodwinds moan;
Then the green silence of many watercresses;
Dessert, a balalaika, strummed alone;
Coffee, a slow, low singing no passion stresses;
Such are my thoughts as - clang! crash! bang! - I brood
And gorge the sticky mess these fools call food!

The Hemp

(A Virginia Legend.)

The Planting of the Hemp.

Captain Hawk scourged clean the seas
(Black is the gap below the plank)
From the Great North Bank to the Caribbees
(Down by the marsh the hemp grows rank).

His fear was on the seaport towns,
The weight of his hand held hard the downs.
And the merchants cursed him, bitter and black,
For a red flame in the sea-fog's wrack
Was all of their ships that might come back.

For all he had one word alone,
One clod of dirt in their faces thrown,
"The hemp that shall hang me is not grown!"

His name bestrode the seas like Death.
The waters trembled at his breath.

This is the tale of how he fell,
Of the long sweep and the heavy swell,
And the rope that dragged him down to hell.

The fight was done, and the gutted ship,
Stripped like a shark the sea-gulls strip,

Lurched blindly, eaten out with flame,
Back to the land from where she came,
A skimming horror, an eyeless shame.

And Hawk stood upon his quarter-deck,

And saw the sky and saw the wreck.

Below, a butt for sailors' jeers,
White as the sky when a white squall nears,
Huddled the crowd of the prisoners.

Over the bridge of the tottering plank,
Where the sea shook and the gulf yawned blank,
They shrieked and struggled and dropped and sank,

Pinioned arms and hands bound fast.
One girl alone was left at last.

Sir Henry Gaunt was a mighty lord.
He sat in state at the Council board;
The governors were as nought to him.
From one rim to the other rim

Of his great plantations, flung out wide
Like a purple cloak, was a full month's ride.

Life and death in his white hands lay,
And his only daughter stood at bay,
Trapped like a hare in the toils that day.

He sat at wine in his gold and his lace,
And far away, in a bloody place,
Hawk came near, and she covered her face.

He rode in the fields, and the hunt was brave,
And far away his daughter gave
A shriek that the seas cried out to hear,
And he could not see and he could not save.

Her white soul withered in the mire
As paper shrivels up in fire,
And Hawk laughed, and he kissed her mouth,
And her body he took for his desire.

The Growing of the Hemp.

Sir Henry stood in the manor room,
And his eyes were hard gems in the gloom.

And he said, "Go dig me furrows five
Where the green marsh creeps like a thing alive
There at its edge, where the rushes thrive."

And where the furrows rent the ground,

He sowed the seed of hemp around.

And the blacks shrink back and are sore afraid
At the furrows five that rib the glade,
And the voodoo work of the master's spade.

For a cold wind blows from the marshland near,
And white things move, and the night grows drear,
And they chatter and crouch and are sick with fear.

But down by the marsh, where the gray slaves glean,
The hemp sprouts up, and the earth is seen
Veiled with a tenuous mist of green.

And Hawk still scourges the Caribbees,
And many men kneel at his knees.

Sir Henry sits in his house alone,
And his eyes are hard and dull like stone.

And the waves beat, and the winds roar,
And all things are as they were before.

And the days pass, and the weeks pass,
And nothing changes but the grass.

But down where the fireflies are like eyes,
And the damps shudder, and the mists rise,
The hemp-stalks stand up toward the skies.

And down from the poop of the pirate ship
A body falls, and the great sharks grip.

Innocent, lovely, go in grace!
At last there is peace upon your face.

And Hawk laughs loud as the corpse is thrown,
"The hemp that shall hang me is not grown!"

Sir Henry's face is iron to mark,
And he gazes ever in the dark.

And the days pass, and the weeks pass,
And the world is as it always was.

But down by the marsh the sickles beam,
Glitter on glitter, gleam on gleam,
And the hemp falls down by the stagnant stream.

And Hawk beats up from the Caribbees,
Swooping to pounce in the Northern seas.

Sir Henry sits sunk deep in his chair,
And white as his hand is grown his hair.

And the days pass, and the weeks pass,
And the sands roll from the hour-glass.

But down by the marsh in the blazing sun
The hemp is smoothed and twisted and spun,
The rope made, and the work done.

The Using of the Hemp.

Captain Hawk scourged clean the seas
(Black is the gap below the plank)
From the Great North Bank to the Caribbees
(Down by the marsh the hemp grows rank).

He sailed in the broad Atlantic track,
And the ships that saw him came not back.

And once again, where the wide tides ran,
He stooped to harry a merchantman.

He bade her stop. Ten guns spake true
From her hidden ports, and a hidden crew,
Lacking his great ship through and through.

Dazed and dumb with the sudden death,
He scarce had time to draw a breath

Before the grappling-irons bit deep,
And the boarders slew his crew like sheep.

Hawk stood up straight, his breast to the steel;
His cutlass made a bloody wheel.

His cutlass made a wheel of flame.
They shrank before him as he came.

And the bodies fell in a choking crowd,
And still he thundered out aloud,

"The hemp that shall hang me is not grown!"
They fled at last. He was left alone.

Before his foe Sir Henry stood.
"The hemp is grown, and my word made good!"

And the cutlass clanged with a hissing whir
On the lashing blade of the rapier.

Hawk roared and charged like a maddened buck.
As the cobra strikes, Sir Henry struck,

Pouring his life in a single thrust,
And the cutlass shivered to sparks and dust.

Sir Henry stood on the blood-stained deck,
And set his foot on his foe's neck.

Then from the hatch, where the rent decks slope,
Where the dead roll and the wounded grope,
He dragged the serpent of the rope.

The sky was blue, and the sea was still,
The waves lapped softly, hill on hill,
And between one wave and another wave
The doomed man's cries were little and shrill.

The sea was blue, and the sky was calm;
The air dripped with a golden balm.
Like a wind-blown fruit between sea and sun,
A black thing writhed at a yard-arm.

Slowly then, and awesomely,
The ship sank, and the gallows-tree,
And there was nought between sea and sun
Nought but the sun and the sky and the sea.

But down by the marsh where the fever breeds,
Only the water chuckles and pleads;
For the hemp clings fast to a dead man's throat,
And blind Fate gathers back her seeds.

Poor Devil!

Well, I was tired of life; the silly folk,
The tiresome noises, all the common things
I loved once, crushed me with an iron yoke.
I longed for the cool quiet and the dark,
Under the common sod where louts and kings
Lie down, serene, unheeding, careless, stark,
Never to rise or move or feel again,
Filled with the ecstasy of being dead....

I put the shining pistol to my head
And pulled the trigger hard - I felt no pain,

No pain at all; the pistol had missed fire
I thought; then, looking at the floor, I saw
My huddled body lying there - and awe
Swept over me. I trembled - and looked up.
About me was - not that, my heart's desire,
That small and dark abode of death and peace
But all from which I sought a vain release!
The sky, the people and the staring sun
Glared at me as before. I was undone.
My last state ten times worse than was my first.
Helpless I stood, befooled, betrayed, accursed,
Fettered to Life forever, horribly;
Caught in the meshes of Eternity,
No further doors to break or bars to burst!

Ghosts of a Lunatic Asylum

Here, where men's eyes were empty and as bright
As the blank windows set in glaring brick,
When the wind strengthens from the sea - and night
Drops like a fog and makes the breath come thick;

By the deserted paths, the vacant halls,
One may see figures, twisted shades and lean,
Like the mad shapes that crawl an Indian screen,
Or paunchy smears you find on prison walls.

Turn the knob gently! There's the Thumbless Man,
Still weaving glass and silk into a dream,
Although the wall shows through him - and the Khan
Journeys Cathay beside a paper stream.

A Rabbit Woman chitters by the door
Chilly the grave-smell comes from the turned sod
Come - lift the curtain - and be cold before
The silence of the eight men who were God!

The White Peacock

(France - Ancient Regime.)

I.

Go away!

Go away; I will not confess to you!

His black biretta clings like a hangman's cap; under his twitching fingers
the beads shiver and click,
As he mumbles in his corner, the shadow deepens upon him;
I will not confess!...

Is he there or is it intenser shadow?
Dark huddled coilings from the obscene depths,
Black, formless shadow,
Shadow.
Doors creak; from secret parts of the chateau come the scuffle and worry of rats.

Orange light drips from the guttering candles,
Eddying over the vast embroideries of the bed
Stirring the monstrous tapestries,
Retreating before the sable impending gloom of the canopy
With a swift thrust and sparkle of gold,
Lipping my hands,
Then
Rippling back abashed before the ominous silences
Like the swift turns and starts of an overpowered fencer
Who sees before him Horror
Behind him darkness,
Shadow.

The clock jars and strikes, a thin, sudden note like the sob of a child.
Clock, buhl clock that ticked out the tortuous hours of my birth,
Clock, evil, wizened dwarf of a clock, how many years of agony
have you relentlessly measured,
Yardstick of my stifling shroud?

I am Aumaury de Montreuil; once quick, soon to be eaten of worms.
You hear, Father? Hsh, he is asleep in the night's cloak.

Over me too steals sleep.
Sleep like a white mist on the rotting paintings of cupids and gods
on the ceiling;
Sleep on the carven shields and knots at the foot of the bed,
Oozing, blurring outlines, obliterating colors,
Death.

Father, Father, I must not sleep!
It does not hear - that shadow crouched in the corner...
Is it a shadow?
One might think so indeed, save for the calm face, yellow as wax,
that lifts like the face of a drowned man from the choking darkness.

II.

Out of the drowsy fog my body creeps back to me.

It is the white time before dawn.
Moonlight, watery, pellucid, lifeless, ripples over the world.
The grass beneath it is gray; the stars pale in the sky.
The night dew has fallen;
An infinity of little drops, crystals from which all light has been taken,
Glint on the sighing branches.
All is purity, without color, without stir, without passion.

Suddenly a peacock screams.

My heart shocks and stops;
Sweat, cold corpse-sweat
Covers my rigid body.
My hair stands on end. I cannot stir. I cannot speak.
It is terror, terror that is walking the pale sick gardens
And the eyeless face no man may see and live!
Ah-h-h-h-h!
Father, Father, wake! wake and save me!
In his corner all is shadow.

Dead things creep from the ground.
It is so long ago that she died, so long ago!
Dust crushes her, earth holds her, mold grips her.
Fiends, do you not know that she is dead?...
"Let us dance the pavon!" she said; the waxlights glittered like swords
on the polished floor.
Twinkling on jewelled snuffboxes, beaming savagely from the crass gold
of candelabra,
From the white shoulders of girls and the white powdered wigs of men...
All life was that dance.
The mocking, resistless current,
The beauty, the passion, the perilous madness
As she took my hand, released it and spread her dresses like petals,
Turning, swaying in beauty,
A lily, bowed by the rain,
Moonlight she was, and her body of moonlight and foam,
And her eyes stars.
Oh the dance has a pattern!
But the clear grace of her thrilled through the notes of the viols,
Tremulous, pleading, escaping, immortal, untamed,
And, as we ended,
She blew me a kiss from her hand like a drifting white blossom
And the starshine was gone; and she fled like a bird up the stair.

Underneath the window a peacock screams,
And claws click, scrape
Like little lacquered boots on the rough stone.

Oh the long fantasy of the kiss; the ceaseless hunger, ceaselessly,
divinely appeased!
The aching presence of the beloved's beauty!

The wisdom, the incense, the brightness!

Once more on the ice-bright floor they danced the pavon
But I turned to the garden and her from the lighted candles.
Softly I trod the lush grass between the black hedges of box.
Softly, for I should take her unawares and catch her arms,
And embrace her, dear and startled.

By the arbor all the moonlight flowed in silver
And her head was on his breast.
She did not scream or shudder
When my sword was where her head had lain
In the quiet moonlight;
But turned to me with one pale hand uplifted,
All her satins fiery with the starshine,
Nacreous, shimmering, weeping, iridescent,
Like the quivering plumage of a peacock...
Then her head drooped and I gripped her hair,
Oh soft, scented cloud across my fingers!
Bending her white neck back....

Blood writhed on my hands; I trod in blood....
Stupidly agaze
At that crumpled heap of silk and moonlight,
Where like twitching pinions, an arm twisted,
Palely, and was still
As the face of chalk.

The buhl clock strikes.
Thirty years. Christ, thirty years!
Agony. Agony.

Something stirs in the window,
Shattering the moonlight.
White wings fan.
Father, Father!

All its plumage fiery with the starshine,
Nacreous, shimmering, weeping, iridescent,
It drifts across the floor and mounts the bed,
To the tap of little satin shoes.
Gazing with infernal eyes.
Its quick beak thrusting, rending, devil's crimson...
Screams, great tortured screams shake the dark canopy.
The light flickers, the shadow in the corner stirs;
The wax face lifts; the eyes open.

A thin trickle of blood worms darkly against the vast red coverlet and spreads to a pool on the floor.

Colors

(For D. M. C.)

The little man with the vague beard and guise
Pulled at the wicket. "Come inside!" he said,
"I'll show you all we've got now - it was size
You wanted? - oh, dry colors! Well" - he led
To a dim alley lined with musty bins,
And pulled one fiercely. Violent and bold
A sudden tempest of mad, shrieking sins
Scarlet screamed out above the battered gold
Of tins and picture-frames. I held my breath.
He tugged another hard - and sapphire skies
Spread in vast quietude, serene as death,
O'er waves like crackled turquoise - and my eyes
Burnt with the blinding brilliance of calm sea!
"We're selling that lot there out cheap!" said he.

A Minor Poet

I am a shell. From me you shall not hear
The splendid tramplings of insistent drums,
The orbed gold of the viol's voice that comes,
Heavy with radiance, languorous and clear.
Yet, if you hold me close against the ear,
A dim, far whisper rises clamorously,
The thunderous beat and passion of the sea,
The slow surge of the tides that drown the mere.

Others with subtle hands may pluck the strings,
Making even Love in music audible,
And earth one glory. I am but a shell
That moves, not of itself, and moving sings;
Leaving a fragrance, faint as wine new-shed,
A tremulous murmur from great days long dead.

The Lover in Hell

Eternally the choking steam goes up
From the black pools of seething oil....
How merry
Those little devils are! They've stolen the pitchfork
From Bel, there, as he slept... Look! - oh look, look!
They've got at Nero! Oh it isn't fair!
Lord, how he squeals! Stop it... it's, well - indecent!
But funny!... See, Bel's waked. They'll catch it now!

... Eternally that stifling reek arises,
Blotting the dome with smoky, terrible towers,
Black, strangling trees, whispering obscene things
Amongst their branches, clutching with maimed hands,
Or oozing slowly, like blind tentacles
Up to the gates; higher than that heaped brick
Man piled to smite the sun. And all around
Are devils. One can laugh... but that hunched shape
The face one stone, like those Assyrian kings!
One sees in carvings, watching men flayed red
Horribly laughable in leaps and writhes;
That face - utterly evil, clouded round
With evil like a smoke - it turns smiles sour!
... And Nero there, the flabby cheeks astrain
And sweating agony... long agony...
Imperishable, unappeasable
For ever... well... it droops the mouth. Till I
Look up.
There's one blue patch no smoke dares touch.
Sky, clear, ineffable, alive with light,
Always the same...
Before, I never knew
Rest and green peace.
She stands there in the sun.
... It seems so quaint she should have long gold wings.
I never have got used - folded across
Her breast, or fluttering with fierce, pure light,
Like shaken steel. Her crown too. Well, it's queer!
And then she never cared much for the harp
On earth. Here, though...
She is all peace, all quiet,
All passionate desires, the eloquent thunder
Of new, glad suns, shouting aloud for joy,
Over fresh worlds and clean, trampling the air
Like stooping hawks, to the long wind of horns,
Flung from the bastions of Eternity...
And she is the low lake, drowsy and gentle,
And good words spoken from the tongues of friends,
And calmness in the evening, and deep thoughts,
Falling like dreams from the stars' solemn mouths.
All these.
They said she was unfaithful once.
Or I remembered it - and so, for that,
I lie here, I suppose. Yes, so they said.
You see she is so troubled, looking down,
Sorrowing deeply for my torments. I
Of course, feel nothing while I see her - save
That sometimes when I think the matter out,
And what earth-people said of us, of her,
It seems as if I must be, here, in heaven,

And she
... Then I grow proud; and suddenly
There comes a splatter of oil against my skin,
Hurting this time. And I forget my pride:
And my face writhes.
Some day the little ladder
Of white words that I build up, up, to her
May fetch me out. Meanwhile it isn't bad....

But what a sense of humor God must have!

Winged Man

The moon, a sweeping scimitar, dipped in the stormy straits,
The dawn, a crimson cataract, burst through the eastern gates,
The cliffs were robed in scarlet, the sands were cinnabar,
Where first two men spread wings for flight and dared the hawk afar.

There stands the cunning workman, the crafty past all praise,
The man who chained the Minotaur, the man who built the Maze.
His young son is beside him and the boy's face is a light,
A light of dawn and wonder and of valor infinite.

Their great vans beat the cloven air, like eagles they mount up,
Motes in the wine of morning, specks in a crystal cup,
And lest his wings should melt apace old Daedalus flies low,
But Icarus beats up, beats up, he goes where lightnings go.

He cares no more for warnings, he rushes through the sky,
Braving the crags of ether, daring the gods on high,
Black 'gainst the crimson sunset, golden o'er cloudy snows,
With all Adventure in his heart the first winged man arose.

Dropping gold, dropping gold, where the mists of morning rolled,
On he kept his way undaunted, though his breaths were stabs of cold,
Through the mystery of dawning that no mortal may behold.

Now he shouts, now he sings in the rapture of his wings,
And his great heart burns intenser with the strength of his desire,
As he circles like a swallow, wheeling, flaming, gyre on gyre.

Gazing straight at the sun, half his pilgrimage is done,
And he staggers for a moment, hurries on, reels backward, swerves
In a rain of scattered feathers as he falls in broken curves.

Icarus, Icarus, though the end is piteous,
Yet forever, yea, forever we shall see thee rising thus,
See the first supernal glory, not the ruin hideous.

You were Man, you who ran farther than our eyes can scan,
Man absurd, gigantic, eager for impossible Romance,
Overthrowing all Hell's legions with one warped and broken lance.

On the highest steeps of Space he will have his dwelling-place,
In those far, terrific regions where the cold comes down like Death
Gleams the red glint of his pinions, smokes the vapor of his breath.

Floating downward, very clear, still the echoes reach the ear
Of a little tune he whistles and a little song he sings,
Mounting, mounting still, triumphant, on his torn and broken wings!

Music

My friend went to the piano; spun the stool
A little higher; left his pipe to cool;
Picked up a fat green volume from the chest;
And propped it open.
Whitely without rest,
His fingers swept the keys that flashed like swords,
... And to the brute drums of barbarian hordes,
Roaring and thunderous and weapon-bare,
An army stormed the bastions of the air!
Dreadful with banners, fire to slay and parch,
Marching together as the lightnings march,
And swift as storm-clouds. Brazen helms and cars
Clanged to a fierce resurgence of old wars
Above the screaming horns. In state they passed,
Trampling and splendid on and sought the vast
Rending the darkness like a leaping knife,
The flame, the noble pageant of our life!
The burning seal that stamps man's high indenture
To vain attempt and most forlorn adventure;
Romance, and purple seas, and toppling towns,
And the wind's valiance crying o'er the downs;
That nerves the silly hand, the feeble brain,
From the loose net of words to deeds again
And to all courage! Perilous and sharp
The last chord shook me as wind shakes a harp!
... And my friend swung round on his stool, and from gods we were men,
"How pretty!" we said; and went on with our talk again.

The Innovator

(A Pharaoh Speaks.)

I said, "Why should a pyramid

Stand always dully on its base?
I'll change it! Let the top be hid,
The bottom take the apex-place!"
And as I bade they did.

The people flocked in, scores on scores,
To see it balance on its tip.
They praised me with the praise that bores,
My godlike mind on every lip.
Until it fell, of course.

And then they took my body out
From my crushed palace, mad with rage,
Well, half the town WAS wrecked, no doubt
Their crazy anger to assuage
By dragging it about.

The end? Foul birds defile my skull.
The new king's praises fill the land.
He clings to precept, simple, dull;
HIS pyramids on bases stand.
But - Lord, how usual!

Love in Twilight

There is darkness behind the light - and the pale light drips
Cold on vague shapes and figures, that, half-seen loom
Like the carven prows of proud, far-triumphing ships
And the firelight wavers and changes about the room,

As the three logs crackle and burn with a small still sound;
Half-blotting with dark the deeper dark of her hair,
Where she lies, head pillowed on arm, and one hand curved round
To shield the white face and neck from the faint thin glare.

Gently she breathes - and the long limbs lie at ease,
And the rise and fall of the young, slim, virginal breast
Is as certain-sweet as the march of slow wind through trees,
Or the great soft passage of clouds in a sky at rest.

I kneel, and our arms enlace, and we kiss long, long.
I am drowned in her as in sleep. There is no more pain.
Only the rustle of flames like a broken song
That rings half-heard through the dusty halls of the brain.

One shaking and fragile moment of ecstasy,
While the grey gloom flutters and beats like an owl above.
And I would not move or speak for the sea or the sky
Or the flame-bright wings of the miraculous Dove!

The Fiddling Wood

Gods, what a black, fierce day! The clouds were iron,
Wrenched to strange, rugged shapes; the red sun winked
Over the rough crest of the hairy wood
In angry scorn; the grey road twisted, kinked,
Like a sick serpent, seeming to environ
The trees with magic. All the wood was still

Cracked, crannied pines bent like malicious cripples
Before the gusty wind; they seemed to nose,
Nudge, poke each other, cackling with ill mirth
Enchantment's days were over - sh! - Suppose
That crouching log there, where the white light stipples
Should - break its quiet! WAS THAT CRIMSON - EARTH?

It smirched the ground like a lewd whisper, "Danger!"
I hunched my cloak about me - then, appalled,
Turned ice and fire by turns - for - someone stirred
The brown, dry needles sharply! Terror crawled
Along my spine, as forth there stepped - a Stranger!
And all the pines crooned like a drowsy bird!

His stock was black. His great shoe-buckles glistened.
His fur cuffs ended in a sheen of rings.
And underneath his coat a case bulged blackly
He swept his beaver in a rush of wings!
Then took the fiddle out, and, as I listened,
Tightened and tuned the yellowed strings, hung slackly.

Ping! Pang! The clear notes swooped and curved and darted,
Rising like gulls. Then, with a finger skinny,
He rubbed the bow with rosin, said, "Your pardon
Signor! Maestro Nicolo Paganini
They used to call me! Tchk! - The cold grips hard on
A poor musician's fingers!" - His lips parted.

A tortured soul screamed suddenly and loud,
From the brown, quivering case! Then, faster, faster,
Dancing in flame-like whorls, wild, beating, screaming,
The music wailed unutterable disaster;
Heartbroken murmurs from pale lips once proud,
Dead, choking moans from hearts once nobly dreaming.

Till all resolved in anguish - died away
Upon one minor chord, and was resumed
In anguish; fell again to a low cry,
Then rose triumphant where the white fires fumed,

Terrible, marching, trampling, reeling, gay,
Hurling mad, broken legions down to die

Through everlasting hells - The tears were salt
Upon my fingers - Then, I saw, behind
The fury of the player, all the trees
Crouched like violinists, boughs crooked, jerking, blind,
Sweeping mad bows to music without fault,
Grey cheeks to greyer fiddles, withered knees.

Gasping, I fled! - but still that devilish tune
Stunned ears and brain alike - till clouds of dust
Blotted the picture, and the noise grew dim
Shaking, I reached the town - and turned - in trust
Wind-smitten, dread, against the sky-line's rim,
Black, dragon branches whipped below a moon!

Portrait of a Boy

After the whipping he crawled into bed,
Accepting the harsh fact with no great weeping.
How funny uncle's hat had looked striped red!
He chuckled silently. The moon came, sweeping
A black, frayed rag of tattered cloud before
In scorning; very pure and pale she seemed,
Flooding his bed with radiance. On the floor
Fat motes danced. He sobbed, closed his eyes and dreamed.

Warm sand flowed round him. Blurts of crimson light
Splashed the white grains like blood. Past the cave's mouth
Shone with a large, fierce splendor, wildly bright,
The crooked constellations of the South;
Here the Cross swung; and there, affronting Mars,
The Centaur stormed aside a froth of stars.
Within, great casks, like wattled aldermen,
Sighed of enormous feasts, and cloth of gold
Glowed on the walls like hot desire. Again,
Beside webbed purples from some galleon's hold,
A black chest bore the skull and bones in white
Above a scrawled "Gunpowder!" By the flames,
Decked out in crimson, gemmed with syenite,
Hailing their fellows with outrageous names,
The pirates sat and diced. Their eyes were moons.
"Doubloons!" they said. The words crashed gold. "Doubloons!"

Portrait of a Baby

He lay within a warm, soft world
Of motion. Colors bloomed and fled,
Maroon and turquoise, saffron, red,
Wave upon wave that broke and whirled
To vanish in the grey-green gloom,
Perspectiveless and shadowy.
A bulging world that had no walls,
A flowing world, most like the sea,
Compassing all infinity
Within a shapeless, ebbing room,
An endless tide that swells and falls...
He slept and woke and slept again.
As a veil drops Time dropped away;
Space grew a toy for children's play,
Sleep bolted fast the gates of Sense
He lay in naked impotence;
Like a drenched moth that creeps and crawls
Heavily up brown, light-baked walls,
To fall in wreck, her task undone,
Yet somehow striving toward the sun.
So, as he slept, his hands clenched tighter,
Shut in the old way of the fighter,
His feet curled up to grip the ground,
His muscles tautened for a bound;
And though he felt, and felt alone,
Strange brightness stirred him to the bone,
Cravings to rise - till deeper sleep
Buried the hope, the call, the leap;
A wind puffed out his mind's faint spark.
He was absorbed into the dark.
He woke again and felt a surge
Within him, a mysterious urge
That grew one hungry flame of passion;
The whole world altered shape and fashion.
Deceived, befooled, bereft and torn,
He scourged the heavens with his scorn,
Lifting a bitter voice to cry
Against the eternal treachery
Till, suddenly, he found the breast,
And ceased, and all things were at rest,
The earth grew one warm languid sea
And he a wave. Joy, tingling, crept
Throughout him. He was quenched and slept.

So, while the moon made broad her ring,
He slept and cried and was a king.
So, worthily, he acted o'er
The endless miracle once more.
Facing immense adventures daily,
He strove still onward, weeping, gaily,
Conquered or fled from them, but grew

As soil-starved, rough pine-saplings do.
Till, one day, crawling seemed suspect.
He gripped the air and stood erect
And splendid. With immortal rage
He entered on man's heritage!

"Ah, did you once see Shelley plain?"
Browning.

"Shelley? Oh, yes, I saw him often then,"
The old man said. A dry smile creased his face
With many wrinkles. "That's a great poem, now!
That one of Browning's! Shelley? Shelley plain?
The time that I remember best is this

A thin mire crept along the rutted ways,
And all the trees were harried by cold rain
That drove a moment fiercely and then ceased,
Falling so slow it hung like a grey mist
Over the school. The walks were like blurred glass.
The buildings reeked with vapor, black and harsh
Against the deepening darkness of the sky;
And each lamp was a hazy yellow moon,
Filling the space about with golden motes,
And making all things larger than they were.
One yellow halo hung above a door,
That gave on a black passage. Round about
Struggled a howling crowd of boys, pell-mell,
Pushing and jostling like a stormy sea,
With shouting faces, turned a pasty white
By the strange light, for foam. They all had clods,
Or slimy balls of mud. A few gripped stones.
And there, his back against the battered door,
His pile of books scattered about his feet,
Stood Shelley while two others held him fast,
And the clods beat upon him. `Shelley! Shelley!'
The high shouts rang through all the corridors,
`Shelley! Mad Shelley! Come along and help!'
And all the crowd dug madly at the earth,
Scratching and clawing at the streaming mud,
And fouled each other and themselves. And still
Shelley stood up. His eyes were like a flame
Set in some white, still room; for all his face
Was white, a whiteness like no human color,
But white and dreadful as consuming fire.
His hands shook now and then, like slender cords
Which bear too heavy weights. He did not speak.

So I saw Shelley plain."
"And you?" I said.

"I? I threw straighter than the most of them,
And had firm clods. I hit him - well, at least
Thrice in the face. He made good sport that night."

Road and Hills

I shall go away
To the brown hills, the quiet ones,
The vast, the mountainous, the rolling,
Sun-fired and drowsy!

My horse snuffs delicately
At the strange wind;
He settles to a swinging trot; his hoofs tramp the dust.
The road winds, straightens,
Slashes a marsh,
Shoulders out a bridge,
Then -
Again the hills.
Unchanged, innumerable,
Bowing huge, round backs;
Holding secret, immense converse:
In gusty voices,
Fruitful, fecund, toiling
Like yoked black oxen.

The clouds pass like great, slow thoughts
And vanish
In the intense blue.

My horse lopes; the saddle creaks and sways.
A thousand glittering spears of sun slant from on high.
The immensity, the spaces,
Are like the spaces
Between star and star.

The hills sleep.
If I put my hand on one,
I would feel the vast heave of its breath.
I would start away before it awakened
And shook the world from its shoulders.
A cicada's cry deepens the hot silence.
The hills open
To show a slope of poppies,
Ardent, noble, heroic,
A flare, a great flame of orange;

Giving sleepy, brittle scent
That stings the lungs.
A creeping wind slips through them like a ferret; they bow and dance,
answering Beauty's voice...

The horse whinnies. I dismount
And tie him to the grey worn fence.
I set myself against the javelins of grass and sun;
And climb the rounded breast,
That flows like a sea-wave.
The summit crackles with heat, there is no shelter, no hollow from
the flagellating glare.

I lie down and look at the sky, shading my eyes.
My body becomes strange, the sun takes it and changes it, it does not feel,
It is like the body of another.
The air blazes. The air is diamond.
Small noises move among the grass...

Blackly,
A hawk mounts, mounts in the inane
Seeking the star-road,
Seeking the end...
But there is no end.

Here, in this light, there is no end....

Elegy For an Enemy

(For G. H.)

Say, does that stupid earth
Where they have laid her,
Bind still her sullen mirth,
Mirth which betrayed her?
Do the lush grasses hold,
Greenly and glad,
That brittle-perfect gold
She alone had?

Smugly the common crew,
Over their knitting,
Mourn her - as butchers do
Sheep-throats they're slitting!
She was my enemy,
One of the best of them.
Would she come back to me,
God damn the rest of them!

Damn them, the flabby, fat,
Sleek little darlings!
We gave them tit for tat,
Snarlings for snarlings!
Squashy pomposities,
Shocked at our violence,
Let not one tactful hiss
Break her new silence!

Maids of antiquity,
Look well upon her;
Ice was her chastity,
Spotless her honor.
Neighbors, with breasts of snow,
Dames of much virtue,
How she could flame and glow!
Lord, how she hurt you!

She was a woman, and
Tender - at times!
(Delicate was her hand)
One of her crimes!
Hair that strayed elfinly,
Lips red as haws,
You, with the ready lie,
Was that the cause?

Rest you, my enemy,
Slain without fault,
Life smacks but tastelessly
Lacking your salt!
Stuck in a bog whence naught
May catapult me,
Come from the grave, long-sought,
Come and insult me!

WE knew that sugared stuff
Poisoned the other;
Rough as the wind is rough,
Sister and brother!
Breathing the ether clear
Others forlorn have found
Oh, for that peace austere
She and her scorn have found!

www.ingramcontent.com/pod-product-compliance
Lightning Source LLC
Chambersburg PA
CBHW060059050426
42448CB00011B/2535